Selected Opera Arias
TENOR

*10 Essential Arias with Plot Notes, International Phonetic Alphabet,
Recorded Diction Lessons and Recorded Accompaniments*

Extracted from the *G. Schirmer Opera Anthology*, edited by Robert L. Larsen

Translations
Martha Gerhart

International Phonetic Alphabet
Martha Gerhart, Italian and French
Irene Spiegelman, German
David Ivanov, Russian

Diction Recordings
Corradina Caporello, Italian
Pierre Vallet, French
Irene Spiegelman, German
Gina Levinson, Russian

Each aria text has two recordings: a recitation, and then a slowly spoken diction lesson.

Accompaniment Recordings
Laura Ward, piano

To access companion recorded diction lessons and accompaniments online,
visit: **www.halleonard.com/mylibrary**

Enter Code
4919-6854-6500-0483

ISBN 978-1-4950-3093-2

G. SCHIRMER, Inc.

DISTRIBUTED BY

7777 W. BLUEMOUND RD. P.O. BOX 13819 MILWAUKEE, WI 53213

www.musicsalesclassical.com
www.halleonard.com

RELATED ONLINE RESOURCES

Enter the unique a code on the title page to access the following resources at
www.halleonard.com/mylibrary

1. **Recorded Diction Lessons**

Each aria text is recorded twice:

- A recitation by a native speaker of the text in a sympathetic speaking tone, from which the listener can hear the natural flow of the words

- A slow and deliberate, phrase by phrase diction lesson with the native speaker coach, with the student repeating after the teacher

2. **Recorded Piano Accompaniments**

3. **Instructions for using the International Phonetic Alphabet Transliterations (PDFs)**

The following articles and charts explain the approach used in citing the IPA symbols for consonants and vowels with an English equivalent, and also address any special issues of diction in the language.

- "About the Italian IPA Transliterations" by Martha Gerhart

- "About the French IPA Transliterations" by Martha Gerhart

- "About the German IPA Transliterations" by Irene Spiegelman

- "About the Russian IPA Transliterations" by David Ivanov

CONTENTS

The price of this publication includes access to companion recorded diction lessons and accompaniments online, for download or streaming, using the unique code found on the title page.
Visit **www.halleonard.com/mylibrary** and enter the access code.

NOTES AND TRANSLATIONS

COSÌ FAN TUTTE
(Women Are Like That)
1790
music by Wolfgang Amadeus Mozart
libretto by Lorenzo da Ponte

Un'aura amorosa

from Act I, scene 3
setting: Naples, the 18th century; a house shared by the sisters Fiordiligi and Dorabella
character: Ferrando

Ferrando and Guglielmo, young Neapolitan soldiers, are disguised as Albanians, having consented to go along with a plot devised by their friend Don Alfonso to prove or disprove that their girlfriends can be tempted into faithlessness. Ferrando, after the first chapter in this deception, remains in the garden to reflect on the sustaining powers of love.

Un'aura amorosa del nostro tesoro	*A loving breath from our beloved*
un dolce ristoro al cor porgerà . . .	*will grant sweet solace to the heart . . .*
al cor che nudrito da speme d'amore,	*to the heart which, fed by hope of love,*
d'un esca migliore bisogno non ha.	*has no need for better nourishment.*

DON GIOVANNI
1787
music by Wolfgang Amadeus Mozart
libretto by Lorenzo da Ponte (after Giovanni Bertati's libretto for Giuseppe Gazzaniga's opera *Il convitato di pietra*; also after the Don Juan legends)

Dalla sua pace

from Act I, scene 3
setting: Seville, the 17th century (often played as the 18th century); a village green near a tavern; morning
character: Don Ottavio

Donna Anna seems sure that Don Giovanni has been responsible for the attack on her person as well as the murder of her father. In this aria, written to replace "Il mio tesoro" in the Vienna performance of 1788, Ottavio insists that he will know peace only when his fiancée's tranquility is assured.

Come mai creder deggio	*How should I ever believe*
di sì nero delitto capace un cavaliere!	*a gentleman capable of such a heinous crime?*
Ah, di scoprire il vero	*Ah, to discover the truth*
ogni mezzo si cerchi.	*may every means be sought.*
Io sento in petto	*I hear within the breast*
e di sposo e d'amico	*of both husband and friend*
il dover che mi parla:	*the duty that speaks to me:*
disingannarla voglio,	*I will disabuse her,*

o vendicarla!	or avenge her!

Dalla sua pace la mia dipende.	My peace depends on hers.
Quel che a lei piace	That which pleases her
vita mi rende;	gives me life;
quel che le incresce	that which displeases her
morte mi dà.	kills me.
S'ella sospira,	If she sighs,
sospiro anch'io.	I sigh too.
È mia quell'ira;	That rage is mine;
quel pianto è mio,	that mourning is mine,
e non ho bene	and I do not have joy
s'ella non l'ha.	if she doesn't.

Il mio tesoro

from Act II, scene 2
setting: Seville, the 17th century (often played as the 18th century); a courtyard adjoining Donna Anna's house
character: Don Ottavio

At last Don Ottavio is convinced that Don Giovanni is responsible for the murder of Donna Anna's father. He declares his determination to avenge this wrong and to bring comfort to his beloved.

Il mio tesoro intanto	Go, meanwhile, to console
andate a consolar,	my beloved;
e del bel ciglio il pianto	and try to dry the tears
cercate di asciugar.	from her beautiful eyes.

Ditele che i suoi torti	Tell her that I am going off
a vendicar io vado:	to avenge her wrongs . . .
che sol di stragi e morti	that I will come back
nunzio vogl'io tornar,	messenger only of ravages
sì!	and deaths—yes!

L'ELISIR D'AMORE
(The Elixir of Love)
1832
music by Gaetano Donizetti
libretto by Felice Romani (after Eugène Scribe's libretto for Daniel-François Auber's *Le Philtre*)

Quanto è bella

from Act I, scene 1
setting: near an Italian village, the 19th century; the lawn of Adina's farmhouse, one of her estates; noon on a summer day
character: Nemorino

The simple peasant lad Nemorino is in love with Adina, a wealthy girl of the village. In the first scene of the opera, as peasant workers sit about enjoying a rest from their labors, Nemorino stands aside contrasting Adina's charms and intelligence with his own lack of wit and character.

Quanto è bella, quanto è cara!	*How beautiful she is; how dear she is!*
Più la vedo e più mi piace,	*The more I see her the more she pleases me,*
ma in quel cor non son capace	*but I am not capable of inspiring*
lieve affetto ad inspirar.	*the slightest affection in that heart.*
Essa legge, studia, impara . . .	*She reads, she studies, she learns;*
non vi ha cosa ad essa ignota.	*there is not a thing unknown to her.*
Io son sempre un idiota.	*I am always a fool.*
Io non so che sospirar.	*Sighing is all I know.*
Ma in quel cor non son capace	*But I am not capable of inspiring*
lieve affetto d'inspirar—	*the slightest affection—*
lieve affetto, in quel core	*of inspiring in that heart*
ad inspirer.	*the slightest affection.*

Una furtiva lagrima

from Act II, scene 2
setting: an Italian village, the 19th century; the village square
character: Nemorino

Nemorino thinks that his sudden success with the girls of the village is because he has taken Dr. Dulcamara's elixir. He doesn't know yet, as they do, that he is about to inherit great wealth. As he wanders away from the village dance he only knows that Adina seemed distressed, and that he would gladly die if he could hold her in his arms.

Una furtiva lagrima	*A furtive tear*
negl'occhi suoi spuntò.	*fell from her eyes.*
Quelle festose giovani	*She seemed to envy*
invidiar sembrò.	*those merry girls.*
Che più cercando io vo'?	*What more am I looking for?*
M'ama. Sì, m'ama.	*She loves me. Yes, she loves me.*
Lo vedo.	*I see it.*
Un solo istante i palpiti	*To feel the throbbings of her*
del suo bel cor sentir!	*beautiful heart for a single instant!*
I miei sospir confondere	*To mingle my sighs*
per poco a' suoi sospir!	*for a short time with her sighs!*
I palpiti sentir,	*To feel the throbbings,*
confondere i miei co' suoi sospir!	*to mingle her sighs with mine!*
Cielo, si può morir;	*Heaven, I could die;*
di più non chiedo.	*I ask for nothing more.*
Ah!	*Ah!*

EUGENE ONEGIN
1879
music by Pyotr Il'yich Tchaikovsky
libretto by Konstantin Shilovsky and the composer (after the poem by Alexander Pushkin)

Lenski's Aria
(Kuda, kuda, kuda vy udalilis')

from Act II, scene 2
setting: Russia, the late 19th century; an open area beside a stream; winter; dawn
character: Lenski

Tempers explode at a party in a country house and Lenski challenges his friend Onegin to a duel. As Lenski waits for Onegin to arrive at the appointed hour, he reflects on his youth and wonders what fate now holds in store.

Kuda, kuda, kuda, vy udalilis'	*Where, where, oh where have you fled,*
vesny moej zlatye dni?	*my springtime's golden days?*
Shto den' grjadushchij mne gotovit?	*What will the coming day prepare for me?*
Ego moj vzor naprasno lovit;	*In vain my gaze attempts to grasp it;*
v glubokoj t'me taitsja on!	*in deep darkness it hides itself!*
Net nuzhdy; prav sud'by zakon!	*No matter; fate's law is just!*
Padu li ja streloj pronzënnyj,	*Whether I fall, pierced by the arrow,*
il' mimo proletit ona,	*or whether it flies by,*
vse blago: bdenia i sna	*all's well: of waking and of sleep*
prikhodit chas opredelënnyj!	*comes the appointed hour!*
Blagosloven i den' zabot,	*Blessed is the day of cares,*
blagosloven i t'my prikhod!	*blessed is the fall of darkness!*
Blesnët zautra luch dennitsy	*A ray of dawn will shine tomorrow*
i zaigraet jarkij den',	*and the brilliant day will sparkle,*
a ja, byt' mozhet . . . ja grobnitsy	*but I, perhaps . . . I will descend*
sojdu v tainstvennuju sen'!	*into the tomb's mysterious protection!*
I pamjat' junogo poeta	*And the young poet's memory*
poglotit medlennaja Leta,	*will engulf the slow Lethe,*
zabuet mir menja, no ty!	*the world will forget me, but you!*
ty, Ol'ga!	*you, Olga!*
Skazhi, pridësh' li, deva krasoty,	*Tell me, will you come, maid of beauty,*
slezu prolit' nad rannej urnoj	*to shed a tear over my early urn*
i dumat': on menja ljubil!	*and think: he loved me!*
On mne edinoj posvjatil	*To me alone he consecrated*
raccvet pechal'nyj zhizni burnoj!	*the mournful daybreak of a stormy life!*
akh, Ol'ga, ja tebja ljubil,	*ah Olga, I loved you,*
tebe edinoj posvjatil'	*to you alone I consecrated*
raccvet pechal'nyj zhizni burnoj!	*the mournful daybreak of a stormy life,*
akh, Ol'ga, ja tebja ljubil!	*ah Olga, I loved you!*
Serdechnyj drug, zhelannyj drug,	*Beloved friend, desired friend,*
pridi, pridi!	*come, come!*
Zhelannjy drug,	*Desired friend.*
pridi, ja tvoj suprug,	*come, I am your spouse,*
pridi, pridi!	*come, come!*
Ja zhdu tebja, zhelannyj drug.	*I wait for you, desired friend.*
Pridi, pridi, ja tvoj suprug!	*Come, come, I am your spouse!*
Kuda, kuda, kuda, vy udalilis'	*Where, where, oh where have you fled,*
zlatye dni, zlatye dni moej vesny!	*my golden days, my springtime's golden days?*

Russian translation and transliteration by Lilia Guimaraez

RIGOLETTO
1851
music by Giuseppe Verdi
libretto by Francesco Maria Piave (after Victor Hugo's drama *Le Roi s'Amuse*)

La donna è mobile

from Act III or Act IV, depending on the version played
setting: Mantua, the 16th century; Sparafucile's dilapidated inn on the outskirts of town
character: the Duke of Mantua

In the last scene of the opera, the Duke, disguised as a soldier, enters the inn of the gypsy assassin Sparafucile. He orders wine and, while he is being served, sings this song about the fickleness of women. Verdi knew that the tune would be a sensation and took care that it was not heard outside Venice's Teatro La Fenice before the premiere performance.

La donna è mobile	*Woman is fickle*
qual piuma al vento;	*like a feather in the wind;*
muta d'accento	*she vacillates in word*
e di pensiero.	*and in thought.*
Sempre un amabile	*A lovable,*
leggiadro viso,	*pretty face,*
in pianto o in riso,	*in tears or in laughter,*
è menzognero.	*is always lying.*
E sempre misero	*He who relies upon her,*
chi a lei s'affida,	*who rashly entrusts*
chi le confida	*his heart to her,*
mal cauto il core!	*is always miserable!*
Pur mai non sentesi	*And yet he who does not*
felice appieno	*drink love upon that breast*
chi su quel seno	*never feels*
non liba amore!	*completely happy!*

LE ROI D'YS
(The King of Ys)
1888
music by Edouard Lalo
libretto by Edouard Blau (after a Breton legend)

Vainement, ma bien-aimée

from Act III
setting: Legendary; a gallery in the palace of the King of Ys
character: Mylio

It is the day of the wedding of the King's daughter Rozenn and Mylio. According to Breton custom, the bride's door is guarded by female attendants against entry by the groom's men. Just before the bridal procession, Mylio sings this charming aubade, accompanied by the women's chorus, outside Rozenn's chamber.

Puisqu'on ne peut fléchir	*Since one can not sway*
ces jalouses gardiennes,	*those jealous protectresses,*
ah, laissez-moi conter	*ah, let me tell*
mes peines et mon émoi!	*my sorrows and my feelings!*

Vainement, ma bien-aimée,	*In vain, my beloved,*
on croit me désespérer;	*they think they're making me desperate;*
près de ta porte fermée	*near your closed door*
je veux encor demeurer!	*I still wish to dwell!*
Les soleils pourront s'éteindre,	*The suns will die out,*
les nuits remplacer les jours,	*the nights replace the days,*
sans t'accuser et sans me plaindre.	*before I reproach you and before I complain.*
Là je resterai, toujours!	*There I will remain, forever!*

Je le sais, ton âme est douce,	*I know your soul is sweet,*
et l'heure bientôt viendra	*and the hour will soon come*
où la main qui me repousse	*when the hand that spurns me*
vers la mienne se tendra!	*will reach out toward mine!*
Ne sois pas trop tardive	*Do not be too late*
à te laisser attendrir!	*in letting your heart soften!*
Si Rozenn bientôt n'arrive,	*If Rozenn doesn't come soon,*
je vais, hélas, mourir!	*alas, I'm going to die!*

LA TRAVIATA
(The Fallen Woman)
1853
music by Giuseppe Verdi
libretto by Francesco Maria Piave (after the play *La Dame aux Camélias* by Alexandre Dumas, fils)

De' miei bollenti spiriti

from Act II
setting: near Paris, 1850; a country house
character: Alfredo Germont

In the first act of the opera, the young Alfredo Germont declared his love for the beautiful courtesan Violetta Valery. At the country estate which they now share, he rejoices at his great good fortune in having convinced Violetta to leave the society where she reigned as queen, coming to live with him in harmonious love and deep contentment.

Lunge da lei per me non v'ha diletto!	*Far from her there is no joy for me!*
Volaron già tre lune	*Three months have already flown by*
dacchè la mia Violetta	*since my Violetta*
agi per me lasciò, dovizie, amori	*abandoned for me luxuries, riches, loves*
e le pompose feste,	*and the ostentatious parties*
ov'agli omaggi avvezza,	*where, accustomed to compliments,*
vedea schiavo ciascun	*she saw everyone a slave*
di sua bellezza.	*of her beauty.*
Ed or contenta in questi ameni luoghi	*And now, content in these pleasant surroundings,*
tutto scorda per mie.	*she forgets it all for me.*
Qui presso a lei io rinascer mi sento,	*Here with her I feel myself reborn;*
e dal soffio d'amor rigenerato	*and, revitalized by the breath of love*

| scordo ne' gaudi suoi | *I forget, in its joys,* |
| tutto il passato. | *all the past.* |

De' miei bollenti spiriti	*She tempered the youthful ardor*
il giovanile ardore	*of my burning spirits*
ella temprò col placido	*with her calm smile*
sorriso dell'amor!	*of love!*
Dal dì che disse:	*Since the day that she said,*
vivere io voglio a te fedel, sì,	*"I want to live faithful to you—yes,"*
dell'universo immemore	*unconscious of the universe,*
io vivo quasi in ciel.	*I live almost in paradise.*
Ah sì.	*Ah yes!*

DIE ZAUBERFLÖTE
(The Magic Flute)
1791
music by Wolfgang Amadeus Mozart
libretto by Emanuel Schikaneder (loosely based on a fairy tale by Wieland)

Dies Bildnis ist bezaubernd schön

from Act I, scene 1
setting: Legendary; a wild mountain pass
character: Tamino

The prince Tamino has just been saved from the jaws of a mighty serpent by three ladies from the court of the Queen of the Night. They give him a portrait of the daughter of the queen. He reflects on her beauty and the new emotions that it inspires in him.

Dies Bildnis ist bezaubernd schön,	*This portrait is enchantingly beautiful,*
wie noch kein Auge je gesehn!	*as no eye has ever before beheld!*
Ich fühl' es, wie dies Götterbild	*I feel it—how this godlike image*
mein Herz mit neuer Regung füllt.	*fills my heart with new emotion.*
Dies Etwas kann ich zwar nicht nennen;	*I cannot really name this thing;*
doch fühl ich's hier wie Feuer brennen.	*yet I feel it here, burning like fire.*
Soll die Empfindung Liebe sein?	*Could this sensation be love?*
Ja, ja! Die Liebe ist's allein.	*Yes, yes! It is love alone.*

O wenn ich sie nur finden könnte!	*Oh, if only I could find her!*
O wenn sie doch schon vor mir stände!	*Oh, if only she were already here before me!*
Ich würde . . . warm und rein—	*I would . . . warmly and chastely—*
was würde ich?	*what would I?*
Ich würde sie voll Entzükken	*I would, full of delight,*
an diesen heißen Busen drücken,	*press her to this burning breast;*
und ewig wäre sie dann mein.	*and then she would be forever mine.*

ABOUT THE ITALIAN IPA TRANSLITERATIONS
by Martha Gerhart

While the IPA is currently the diction learning tool of choice for singers not familiar with the foreign languages in which they sing, differences in transliterations exist in diction manuals and on the internet, just as differences of pronunciation exist in the Italian language itself.

The Italian transliterations in this volume reflect the following choices:

All unstressed "e's" and "o's" are *closed*. This choice is based on the highest form of the spoken language, as in the authoritative Italian dictionary edited by Zingarelli. However, in practice, singers may well make individual choices as to *closed* or *open* depending upon the vocal tessitura and technical priorities.

Also, there are many Italian words (such as "sento," "cielo," and etc.) for which, in practice, both *closed* and *open* vowels in the *stressed* syllable are perfectly acceptable.

The "nasal 'm'" symbol [ɱ], indicating that the letter "n" assimilates before a "v" or an "f" (such as "inferno" becoming [im ˈfɛr rr] in execution, is not used in these transliterations. This choice was a practical one to avoid confusion on the part of the student who might wonder why "in" is transcribed as if it were "im," unlike in any dictionary. However, students are encouraged to use the [ɱ] as advised by experts.

Double consonants which result, in execution, from *phrasal doubling* (*raddoppiamento sintattico*) are not transliterated as such; but students should utilize this sophistication of Italian lyric diction as appropriate.

The syllabic divisions in these transliterations are in the interest of encouraging the singer to lengthen the vowel before a single consonant rather than making an incorrect double consonant, and also to encourage the singer, when there are two consonants, the first of which is *l, m, n,* or *r,* to give more strength to the first of those two consonants.

Intervocalic "s's" are transliterated as *voiced*, despite the fact that in many words ("casa," "così," etc.) the "s" is *unvoiced* in the language (and in the above-mentioned dictionary). Preferred practice for singers is to *voice* those "s's" in the interest of legato; yet, an unvoiced "s" pronunciation in those cases is not incorrect. (*Note*: words which combine a prefix and a stem beginning with an unvoiced "s" ["risolvi," "risanare," etc.] retain the unvoiced "s" of the prefix in singing as well as in speech.)

Many Italian words have alternate pronunciations given in the best dictionaries, particularly regarding closed or open vowels. In my IPA transliterations I chose the first given pronunciation, which is not always the preferred pronunciation in common Italian usage as spoken by Corradina Caporello on the accompanying recordings. I defer to my respected colleague in all cases for her expert pronunciation of beautiful Italian diction.

Pronunciation Key

IPA Symbol	Approximate sound in English	IPA Symbol	Approximate sound in English
[i]	feet	[s]	set
[e]	potato	[z]	zip
[ɛ]	bed	[l]	lip
[a]	father	[ʎ]	million
[ɔ]	taut		
[o]	tote	[ɾ]	as *British* "very" – flipped "r"
[u]	tube	[r]	no English equivalent – rolled "r"
[j]	Yale		
[w]	watch	[n]	name
		[m]	mop
[b]	beg	[ŋ]	anchor
[p]	pet	[ɲ]	onion
[d]	deep	[tʃ]	cheese
[t]	top	[dʒ]	George
[g]	Gordon	[dz]	feeds
[k]	kit	[ts]	fits
[v]	vet		
[f]	fit	[ː]	indicates doubled consonants
[ʃ]	she	[ˈ]	indicates the primary stress; the syllable following the mark is stressed

ABOUT THE FRENCH IPA TRANSLITERATIONS
by Martha Gerhart

Following is a table of pronunciation for French lyric diction in singing as transliterated in this volume.

THE VOWELS

symbol	nearest equivalent in English	descriptive notes
[ɑ]	as in "father"	the "dark 'a'"
[a]	in English only in dialect; comparable to the Italian "a"	the "bright 'a'"
[e]	no equivalent in English; as in the German "Schnee"	the "closed 'e'": [i] in the [ɛ] position
[ɛ]	as in "bet"	the "open 'e'"
[i]	as in "feet"	
[o]	no equivalent in English as a pure vowel; approximately as in "open"	the "closed 'o'"
[ɔ]	as in "ought"	the "open 'o'"
[u]	as in "blue"	
[y]	no equivalent in English	[i] sustained with the lips rounded to a [u] position
[ø]	no equivalent in English	[e] sustained with the lips rounded almost to [u]
[œ] *	as in "earth" without pronouncing any "r"	[ɛ] with lips in the [ɔ] position
[ɑ̃]	no equivalent in English	the nasal "a": [ɔ] with nasal resonance added
[ɔ̃]	no equivalent in English	the nasal "o": [o] with nasal resonance added
[ɛ̃]	no equivalent in English	the nasal "e": as in English "cat" with nasal resonance added
[œ̃]	no equivalent in English	the nasal "œ": as in English "uh, huh" with nasal resonance added

* Some diction manuals transliterate the neutral, unstressed syllables in French as a "schwa" [ə].
Refer to authoritative published sources concerning such sophistications of French lyric diction.

THE SEMI-CONSONANTS

[ɥ]	no equivalent in English	a [y] in the tongue position of [i] and the lip position of [u]
[j]	as in "ewe," "yes"	a "glide"
[w]	as in "we," "want"	

THE CONSONANTS

[b]	as in "bad"	with a few exceptions
[c]	[k], as in "cart"	with some exceptions
[ç]	as in "sun"	when initial or medial, before *a*, *o*, or *u*
[d]	usually, as in "door"	becomes [t] in liaison
[f]	usually, as in "foot"	becomes [v] in liaison
[g]	usually, as in "gate"	becomes [k] in liaison; see also [ʒ]
[k]	as in "kite"	
[l]	as in "lift"	with some exceptions
[m]	as in "mint"	with a few exceptions
[n]	as in "nose"	with a few exceptions
[ɲ]	as in "onion"	almost always the pronunciation of the "gn" combination
[p]	as in "pass"	except when silent (final) and in a few rare words
[r] *	no equivalent in English	flipped (or occasionally rolled) "r"
[s]	as in "solo"	with exceptions; becomes [z] in liaison
[t]	as in "tooth"	with some exceptions
[v]	as in "voice"	
[x]	[ks] as in "extra," [gz] as in "exist," [z] as in "Oz," or [s] as in "sent"	becomes [z] in liaison
[z]	as in "zone"	with some exceptions
[ʒ]	as in "rouge"	usually, "g" when initial or mediant before *e*, *i*, or *y*; also, "j" in any position
[ʃ]	as in "shoe"	

* The conversational "uvular 'r'" is used in popular French song and cabaret but is not considered appropriate for singing in the classical repertoire.

LIAISON AND ELISION

Liaison is common in French. It is the sounding (linking) of a normally silent final consonant with the vowel (or mute h) beginning the next word. Its use follows certain rules; apart from the rules, the final choice as to whether or not to make a liaison depends on good taste and/or the advice of experts.

Examples of liaison, with their IPA:

les oiseaux   est ici
lɛ‿ zwa zo   ɛ‿ ti si

Elision is the linking of a consonant followed by a final unstressed *e* with the vowel (or mute *h*) beginning the next word.

examples, with their IPA: elle est   votre âme
ɛ‿ lɛ   vɔ‿ trɑ mœ

The linking symbol [‿] is given in these transliterations for both **elision** and for (recommended) **liaisons**.

ABOUT THE GERMAN IPA TRANSLITERATIONS
by Irene Spiegelman

TRANSLATIONS

As every singer has experienced, word-by-word translations are usually awkward, often not understandable, especially in German where the verb usually is split up with one part in second position of the main clause and the rest at the end of the sentence. Sometimes it is a second verb, sometimes it is a little word that looks like a preposition. Since prepositions never come by themselves, these are usually *separable prefixes to the verb*. In order to look up the meaning of the verb this prefix has to be reunited with the verb in order to find the correct meaning in the dictionary. They cannot be looked up by themselves. Therefore, in the word-by-word translation they are marked with [1]) and do not show any words.

Note: In verbs with separable prefixes, the prefix gets the emphasis. If a separable prefix appears at the end of the sentence, it still needs to be stressed and since many of them start with vowels they even might be glottaled for emphasis.

Also, there are many *reflexive verbs* in German that are not reflexive in English, also the reflexive version of a verb in German often means something very different than the meaning found if the verb is looked up by itself. Reflexive pronouns that are grammatically necessary but do not have a meaning by themselves do not show a translation underneath. They are marked with [2]).

Another difference in the use of English and German is that German is using the Present Perfect Tense of the verb where English prefers the use of the Simple Past of the verb. In cases like that, the translation appears under the conjugated part of the verb and none underneath the past participle of the verb at the end of the sentence. Those cases are marked with [3]).

One last note concerning the translations: English uses possessive pronouns much more often then German does. So der/die/das in German have at appropriate points been translated as my/your/his.

PRONUNCIATION (EXTENDED IPA SYMBOLS)

The IPA symbols that have been used for the German arias are basically those used in Langenscheidt dictionaries. Other publications have refined some symbols, but after working with young singers for a long time, I find that they usually don't remember which is which sign when the ones for long closed vowels (a and ɑ, or ʏ and y) are too close, and especially with the signs for the open and closed u-umlauts they usually cannot tell which they handwrote into their scores. To make sure that a vowel should be closed there is ":" behind the symbol, i.e. [byːp laɪn]

After having been encouraged to sing on a vowel as long as possible, often the consonants are cut too short. The rule is, **"Vowels can be used to make your voice shine, consonants will help your interpretation!"** This is very often totally neglected in favor of long vowels, even when the vowels are supposed to be short. Therefore, double consonants show up here in the IPA line. This suggests that they should at least not be neglected. There are voiced consonants on which it is easy to sing (l, m, n) and often give the text an additional dimension. That is not true for explosive consonants (d, t, k), but they open the vowels right in front of them. So the double consonants in these words serve here as reminders. German does not require to double the consonants the way Italian does, but that Italian technique might help to move more quickly to the consonant, and therefore open the vowel or at least don't stretch it, which sometimes turns it into a word with a different meaning altogether.

One idea that is heard over and over again is: "There is no legato in German." The suggestions that are marked here with ⇨ in the IPA line show that **that is not true.** Always elided can be words ending in a vowel with the next word beginning with a vowel. Words that end with a -t sound can be combined with the next word that starts with a t- or a d-. A word ending in -n can be connected to the following beginning -n. But words ending in consonants can also be elided with the next word starting with a vowel. (example: Dann [dan⇨n] könnt' [kœn⇨n⇨] ich [⇨tɪç] mit [mɪt] Fürsten ['fʏr stən] mich ['mɛs⇨sən]). In this example, the arrow symbol suggests to use the double consonant, but also that the end-t in "könnt'" could be used at the beginning of "ich" which makes the word "ich" much less important (which it usually is in German), and could help to shape the words "Fürsten" and "messen" with more importance.

Within the IPA line, sometimes the "⇨" symbol is only at the end of a word and means that combining this word with the next is absolutely possible if it helps the interpretation of the text or the singer does not want to interrupt the beauty of the musical line. The same fact is true if the "⇨" symbol appears within a word and suggests combining syllables. (Since English syllables are viewed differently than German syllables, the IPA line is broken down into German syllables with suggestions for vocal combinations.) The only consonant that should not be combined with the next word is "r," because there are too many combinations that form new words (example: der Eine, the one and only, should not become [de: raɪ nə], the pure one).

One last remark about pronunciation that seems to have become an issue in the last few years: How does one pronounce the a-umlaut = ä. Some singers have been told in their diction classes that ä is pronounced like a closed e. That may be the case in casual language and can be heard on German television. But when the texts that we are dealing with were written the sound was either a long or short open e sound ['mɛ: tçən, ʃpɛːt, 'hɛl tə].

Considering the language, how does one make one's voice shine and still use the text for a sensible interpretation? Look for the words within a phrase that are important to you as the interpreter, as the person who believes what he/she is conveying. In those words use the consonants as extensively as possible. [zzze: llə] and [llli: bə] are usually more expressive than [ze: lə] and [li: bə] , also glottal the beginning vowels. Use the surrounding words for singing legato and show off the voice.

The IPA line not only shows correct pronunciation but is also giving guidelines for interpretation. For instance, R's may be rolled or flipped, or words may be connected or separated at any time as long as they help you with your feeling for the drama of the text. But you are the person who has to decide! Be discriminating! Know what you want to say! Your language will fit with the music perfectly.

THE "R" IN GERMAN DICTION

When most Germans speak an "r" in front of a vowel, it is a sound produced between the far back of the tongue and the uvula, almost like a gargling sound. The r's at the end of syllables take on different sounds and often have a vowel-like quality.

In classical singing, the practice is to use "Italian r's". Since trilling the r at the tip of the tongue seems to be easy for most singers, many texts are rendered with any overdone r's, which are remotely possible. As a result, the r's take over the whole text and diminish the meaning and phrasing of the sentences. By being discriminating in using rolled r's in an opera text, the phrasing, i.e. interpretation, as well as the chance of understanding the sung text can be improved.

Essentially, there are three categories of words with different suggestions about the use of r's:

ALWAYS ROLL THE R	END-R'S IN SHORT ONE-SYLLABLE WORDS	END-R'S IN PREFIXES AND SUFFIXES
a) before vowels: **R**ose ['ro: zə] t**r**agen ['tra: gən] sp**r**echen ['ʃprɛ: xən] T**r**ug [tru:k] füh**r**en ['fy: rən] b) after vowels in the main syllable of the word: be**r**gen ['bɛr gən] He**r**z [hɛrts] Schwe**r**t [ʃve:rt] du**r**ch [dʊrç] gewo**r**ben [gə 'vɔr bən] ha**r**t [hart]	End-r's in short one-syllable words that have a closed vowel can be replaced with a short a-vowel, marked in the IPA line with ª. der [de:ª] er [e:ª] wir [vi:ª] hier [hi:ª] vor [fo:ª] nur [nu:ª] **Note:** **After an a-vowel a replacement of r by ª would not sound. Therefore end-r's after any a should be rolled.** **war [va:r]** **gar [ga:r]**	Prefixes: ver- er- zer- Here, e and r could be pronounced as a schwa-sound, almost like a short open e combined with a very short ª. If desired, the r could also be flipped with one little flip in order not to overpower the main part of the word which is coming up. In the IPA-line this is marked with ʀ. verbergen [fɛʀ 'bɛr gən] erklären [ɛʀ 'klɛ: rən] Suffix: -er These suffixes are most of the time not important for the interpretation of the text. Therefore, the schwa-sound as explained above works in most cases very well. It is marked in the IPA-line with ɚ. e-Suffixes are marked with ə. guter ['gu: tɚ] gute ['gu: tə] Winter ['vɪn tɚ] Meistersinger ['maɪ stɚ sɪ ŋɚ] (compound noun, both parts end in -er)

ABOUT THE RUSSIAN IPA TRANSLITERATIONS
by David Ivanov

Following is a table of pronunciation for Russian diction in singing as transliterated in this volume. While the IPA is currently the diction learning tool of choice for singers not familiar with the foreign languages in which they sing, differences exist in transliterations, just as differences of pronunciation exist in the Russian language itself. Research from authoritative published sources as well as sensitivity to how the words interact with the music should guide the singer to the final result.

THE VOWELS

symbol	nearest equivalent in English	descriptive notes
[ɑ]	arm	
[ɛ]	met	
[i]	heat	
[o]	go	pure [o], not [oʊ]
[u]	put	
[ə]	about	
[ɨ]	not an English sound	pronounce as a throaty form of [i]

THE CONSONANTS

symbol	nearest equivalent in English
[b]	bank
[bʲ]	beautiful
[d]	dog
[dʲ]	adieu (French)
[f]	fat
[fʲ]	fume
[g]	gate
[gʲ]	legume
[k]	can
[kʲ]	cue
[l]	lot
[lʲ]	laugh
[m]	mat
[mʲ]	mule
[n]	not
[nʲ]	news
[p]	pin
[pʲ]	pure
[r]	flipped [r]
[rʲ]	flipped [r] in palatalized position
[s]	sat
[sʲ]	see
[t]	top
[tʲ]	costume
[v]	vat
[vʲ]	review
[x]	ach (German)
[xʲ]	not an English sound
[tʃ]	chair
[ʃtʃ]	mesh chair
[ʃ]	mesh
[ʒ]	measure

INTERNATIONAL PHONETIC ALPHABET TRANSLITERATIONS BY ARIA

COSÌ FAN TUTTE
music: Wolfgang Amadeus Mozart
libretto: Lorenzo da Ponte

Un'aura amorosa

u ˈna u ɾa	a mo ˈro za	del	ˈnɔ stro	te ˈzɔ ɾo
Un'aura	**amorosa**	**del**	**nostro**	**tesoro**
a breath	*loving*	*of the*	*our*	*treasure*

un	ˈdol tʃe	ri ˈstɔ ɾo	al	kɔr	por dʒe ˈra
un	**dolce**	**ristoro**	**al**	**cor**	**porgerà...**
a	*sweet*	*comfort*	*to the*	*heart*	*will give*

al	kɔr	ke	nu ˈdri to	da	ˈspɛ me	da ˈmo ɾe
al	**cor**	**che**	**nudrito**	**da**	**speme**	**d'amore,**
to the	*heart*	*which*	*nourished*	*by*	*hope*	*of love*

dun	ˈe ska	miʎ: ˈʎo ɾe	bi ˈzoɲ: ɲo	non	a
d'un	**esca**	**migliore**	**bisogno**	**non**	**ha.**
of a	*food*	*better*	*need*	*not*	*has*

DON GIOVANNI
music: Wolfgang Amadeus Mozart
libretto: Lorenzo da Ponte (after Giovanni Bertati's libretto for Giuseppe Gazzaniga's *Il convitato di pietra*; also after the Don Juan legends)

Dalla sua pace

ˈko me	ˈma i	ˈkre der	ˈdɛd: dʒo
Come	**mai**	**creder**	**deggio**
how	*ever*	*to believe*	*I must*

di	si	ˈne ɾo	de ˈlit: to	ka ˈpa tʃe	un	ka va ˈljɛ ɾo
di	**sì**	**nero**	**delitto**	**capace**	**un**	**cavaliero!**
of	*so*	*dark*	*crime*	*capable*	*a*	*cavalier*

a	di	sko ˈpri ɾe	il	ˈve ɾo
Ah,	**di**	**scoprire**	**il**	**vero**
ah	*of*	*to discover*	*the*	*truth*

ˈoɲ: ɲi	ˈmɛd: dzo	si ˈtʃer ki
ogni	**mezzo**	**si cerchi.**
every	*means*	*let be searched for*

ˈi o	ˈsɛn to	in	ˈpɛt: to
Io	**sento**	**in**	**petto**
I	*[I] hear*	*in*	*breast*

e	di	ˈspɔ zo	e	da ˈmi ko
e	**di**	**sposo**	**e**	**d'amico**
and	*of*	*husband*	*and*	*of friend*

il	do ˈver	ke	mi	ˈpar la
il	**dover**	**che**	**mi**	**parla:**
the	*duty*	*which*	*to me*	*speaks*

di ziŋ ɡan: ˈnar la	ˈvɔʎ: ʎo
disingannarla	**voglio,**
to disabuse her	*I want*

o	ven di ˈkar la
o	**vendicarla!**
or	*to avenge her*

'dal: la   'su a   'pa tʃe   la   'mi a   di 'pɛn de
Dalla   sua   pace   la   mia   dipende.
on the   her   peace   the   mine   depends

kwel   ke   a   'lɛ i   'pja tʃe
Quel   che   a   lei   piace
that   which   to   her   is pleasing

'vi ta   mi   'rɛn de
vita   mi   rende;
life   to me   gives

kwel   ke   le   iŋ 'kreʃ: ʃe
quel   che   le   incresce
that   which   her   displeases

'mɔr te   mi   da
morte   mi   dà.
death   to me   gives

'sel: la   so 'spi ɾa
S'ella   sospira,
if she   sighs

so 'spi ɾo   aŋ 'ki o
sospiro   anch'io.
I sigh   also I

ɛ   'mi a   kwel: 'li ɾa
È   mia   quell'ira;
is   mine   that wrath

kwel   'pjan to   ɛ   'mi o
quel   pianto   è   mio,
that   weeping   is   mine

e   non   ɔ   'bɛ ne
e   non   ho   bene
and   not   I have   happiness

'sel: la   non   la
s'ella   non   l'ha.
if she   not   it has

Il mio tesoro

il   'mi o   te 'zɔ ɾo   in 'tan to
Il   mio   tesoro   intanto
the   my   treasure   meanwhile

an 'da te   a   kon so 'lar
andate   a   consolar,
go   to   [to] console

e   del   bɛl   'tʃiʎ: ʎo   il   'pjan to
e   del   bel   ciglio   il   pianto
and   from the   beautiful   brow   the   tears

tʃer 'ka te   di   aʃ: ʃu 'gar
cercate   di   asciugar.
seek   of   to wipe dry

'di te le   ke   i   'swɔ i   'tɔr ti
Ditele   che   i   suoi   torti
tell her   that   the   her   wrongs

a ven di 'kar   'i o   'va do
a vendicar   io   vado:
to [to] avenge   I   [I] go

ke sol di 'stra dʒi e 'mɔr ti
che sol di stragi e morti
that only of ravages and deaths

'nun tsjo   vɔʎ: 'ʎi o   tor 'nar
nunzio   vogl'io   tornar,
messenger   want I   to return

si
sì!
yes

L'ELISIR D'AMORE

music: Gaetano Donizetti
libretto: Felice Romani (after Eugène Scribe's libretto for Daniel-François Auber's *Le Philtre*)

Quanto è bella

'kwan to   ɛ   'bɛl: la   'kwan to   ɛ   'ka ɾa
Quanto   è   bella,   quanto   è   cara!
how much   she is   beautiful   how much   she is   dear

pju la 've do e pju mi 'pja tʃe
Più la vedo e più mi piace,
more her I see and more me she pleases

ma iŋ kwel kɔr non son ka 'pa tʃe
ma in quel cor non son capace
but in that heart not I am capable

'ljɛ ve af: 'fɛt: to a din spi 'ɾar
lieve affetto ad inspirar.
slight affection to inspire

'es: sa 'lɛd: dʒe 'stu dja im 'pa ɾa
Essa legge, studia, impara...
she reads studies learns

non vi a 'kɔ za a 'des: sa iɲ: 'ɲɔ ta
non vi ha cosa ad essa ignota.
not here has thing to her unknown

'i o son 'sɛm pre un i 'djɔ ta
Io son sempre un idiota.
I [I] am always an idiot

'i o non sɔ ke so spi 'ɾar
Io non so che sospirar.
I not [I] know but to [to] sigh

ma iŋ kwel kɔr non son ka 'pa tʃe
Ma in quel cor non son capace
but in that heart not I am capable

'ljɛ ve af: 'fɛt: to din spi 'ɾar
lieve affetto d'inspirar —
slight affection [of] to inspire

'ljɛ ve af: 'fɛt: to in kwel 'kɔ ɾe
lieve affetto, in quel core
slight affection in that heart

a din spi 'rar
ad inspirar.
to inspire

Una furtiva lagrima

'u na   fur 'ti va   'la gri ma
Una   furtiva   lagrima
a   furtive   tear

neʎ: 'ʎɔk: ki   'swɔ i   spun 'tɔ
negl'occhi   suoi   spuntò.
in the eyes   hers   rose up

'kwel: le   fe 'sto ze   'dʒo va ni
Quelle   festose   giovani
those   festive   young women

in vi di 'ar   sem 'brɔ
invidiar   sembrò.
to envy   she seemed

ke   pju   tʃer 'kan do   'i o   vɔ
Che   più   cercando   io   vo'?
what   more   looking for   I   [I] go

'ma ma   si   'ma ma
M'ama.   Sì,   m'ama.
me she loves yes   me she loves

lo   've do
Lo   vedo.
it   I see

un   'so lo   i 'stan te   i   'pal pi ti
Un   solo   istante   i   palpiti
a   single   instant   the   palpitations

del   'su o   bɛl   kɔr   sen 'tir
del   suo   bel   cor   sentir!
of the   her   beautiful heart   to feel

i   'mjɛ i   so 'spir   kon 'fon de ɾe
I   miei   sospir   confondere
the   my   sighs   to mix

per   'pɔ ko   a   'swɔ i   so 'spir
per   poco   a'   suoi   sospir!
for   short time with   her   sighs

i   'pal pi ti   sen 'tir
I   palpiti   sentir,
the   palpitations to feel

kon 'fon de ɾe   i   'mjɛ i   ko   'swɔ i   so 'spir
confondere   i   miei   co'   suoi   sospir!
to mix   the   my   with   her   sighs

'tʃɛ lo   si   pwɔ   mo 'rir
Cielo,   si   può   morir;
heaven   one   is able to die

di   pju   non   'kjɛ do
di   più   non   chiedo.
of   more   not   I ask

a
Ah!
ah

EUGENE ONEGIN

music: Pyotr Il'yich Tchaikovsky
libretto: Konstantin Shilovsky and Pyotr Il'yich Tchaikovsky (after a poem by Alexander Pushkin)

Lenski's Aria
(Kuda, kuda, kuda vy udalilis')

ku 'dɑ	ku 'dɑ	ku 'dɑ	vɨ	u dɑ 'lʲi lʲisʲ
Куда,	**куда,**	**куда**	**вы**	**удались**
Where,	*where,*	*to where*	*you*	*have fled*

vʲis 'nɨ		mɑ 'jɛi	zlɑ 'tɨ jə	dnʲi
весны		**моей**	**златые**	**дни?**
of springtime		*my*	*golden*	*days?*

ʃto	dɛnʲ	grʲi 'du ʃtʃi	mnʲɛ	gɑ 'to vʲit
Что	**день**	**грядущий**	**мне**	**готовит?**
What	*day*	*coming*	*for me*	*will prepare?*

ji 'vo	moi	vzor	nɑp 'rɑs nə	lɑ 'vʲitʲ
Его	**мой**	**взор**	**напрасно**	**ловить;**
It	*my*	*glance*	*in vain*	*is grasping;*

v	glu 'bo kəi	tʲmʲɛ	tɑ 'it sʲə	on
в	**глубокой**	**тьме**	**таится**	**он!**
in	*deep*	*darkness*	*is hiding*	*itself!*

nʲɛt	'nuʒ dɨ	prɑf	sudʲ 'bɨ	zɑ 'kon
Нет	**нужды;**	**прав**	**судьбы**	**закон!**
(There is)	*no matter;*	*is just*	*of fate*	*law!*

'pɑ du	lʲi	jɑ	strʲi 'loi	prɑn 'zʲo nːɨ
Паду	**ли**	**я**	**стрелой**	**пронзённый,**
Will fall	*whether*	*I*	*with arrow*	*pierced,*

ilʲ	'mʲi mə	prə lʲi 'tʲitʲ	ɑ 'nɑ
иль	**мимо**	**пролетить**	**она,**
or	*by*	*flies*	*it,*

fsʲo	'blɑ gə	'bdʲɛ nʲi jə	i	snɑ
всё	**благо:**	**бдения**	**и**	**сна**
all	*is well:*	*of waking*	*and*	*sleep*

prʲi 'xo dʲit	tʃɑs	ɑp rʲi dʲi 'lo nːɨ
приходит	**час**	**определённый!**
comes	*hour*	*appointed!*

blə gəs lɑ 'vʲɛn	i	dʲɛnʲ	zɑ 'bot
Благословен	**и**	**день**	**забот,**
Is blessed	*both*	*day*	*of cares,*

blə gəs lɑ 'vʲɛn	i	tʲmɨ	prʲi 'xot
благословен	**и**	**тьмы**	**приход!**
is blessed	*(and)*	*of darkness*	*fall!*

blʲis 'nʲɛt	zɑ 'ut rə	lutʃ	dʲi 'nʲːi tsɨ
Блеснет	**заутра**	**луч**	**денницы**
Will shine	*tomorrow morning*	*ray*	*of dawn*

i zə ig ˈrɑ jit ˈjɑr kʲi dʲɛnʲ
и заиграет яркий день,
and will sparkle brilliant day,

ɑ jɑ bitʲ ˈmo ʒit jɑ grʲɑb ˈnʲi tsɨ
а я, быть может... я гробницы
and I, perhaps may... I of tomb's

sɑi ˈdu f tɑ ˈinst vʲi n:u ju sʲɛnʲ
сойду в таинственную сень!
descend into mysterious protection!

i ˈpɑ mʲətʲ ˈju nə və pɑ ˈɛ tə
И память юного поэта
And memory of young poet

pɑg ˈlo tʲit ˈmʲɛd lʲi n:ə jə ˈlʲɛ tə
поглотит медленная лета,
will engulf slow Lethe,

zɑ ˈbu dʲit mʲir mʲi ˈnʲɑ no tɨ
забудет мнр меня, но ты!
will forget world me, but you!

tɨ ˈolʲ gə
ты, Ольга!
you, Olga!

skɑ ˈʒi prʲi ˈdoʃ lʲi ˈdɛ və krɑ ˈso tɨ
Скажи, придёшь ли, дева красоты,
Tell, will you come, maid of beauty,

slʲi ˈzu prɑ ˈlʲitʲ nɑt ˈrɑ nʲːi ˈur nəi
слезу пролить над ранней урной
tear to shed over early urn

i ˈdu mətʲ on mʲi ˈnʲɑ lʲu ˈbʲil
и думать: он меня любил!
and think: he me loved!

on mnʲɛ ji ˈdʲi nəi pəs vʲi ˈtil
Он мне единой посвятил
He to me alone consecrated

rɑs ˈvʲɛt pʲi ˈtʃɑlʲ nɨ ˈʒiz nʲi ˈbur nəi
рассвет печальный жизни бурной!
daybreak mournful of life stormy!

ɑx ˈolʲ gə jɑ tʲi ˈbʲɑ lʲu ˈbʲil
Ах, Ольга, я тебя любил,
Ah, Olga, I you loved,

tʲi ˈbʲɛ ji ˈdʲi nəi pəs vʲi ˈtʲil
тебе единой посвятил
to you alone consecrated

rɑs ˈvʲɛt pʲi ˈtʃɑlʲ nɨ ˈʒiz nʲi ˈbur nəi
рассвет печальный жизни бурной,
daybreak mournful of life stormy,

ɑx ˈolʲ gə jɑ tʲi ˈbʲɑ lʲu ˈbʲil
ах, Ольга, я тебя любил!
ah, Olga, I you loved!

sʲir ˈdʲɛʃ nɨ   druk   ʒi ˈla n:i   druk
Сердечный   друг,   желанный   друг,
Beloved   friend,   desired   friend,

prʲi ˈdʲi   prʲi ˈdʲi
приди,   приди!
come,   come!

ʒi ˈla n:i   druk
Желанный   друг,
Desired   friend,

prʲi ˈdʲi   ja   tvoi   sup ˈruk
приди,   я   твой   супруг,
come,   I am   your   spouse,

prʲi ˈdʲi   prʲi ˈdʲi
приди,   приди!
come,   come!

ja   ʒdu   tʲi ˈba   ʒi ˈla n:i   druk
Я   жду   тебя,   желанный   друг.
I   wait for   you,   desired   friend.

prʲi ˈdʲi   prʲi ˈdʲi   ja   tvoi   sup ˈruk
Приди,   приди,   я   твой   супруг!
Come,   come,   I am   your   spouse!

ku ˈda   ku ˈda   ku ˈda   vɨ   u da ˈlʲi lʲisʲ
Куда,   куда,   куда   вы   удалились,
Where,   where,   to where   you   have fled,

zla ˈtɨ jə   dnʲi   zla ˈtɨ jə   dnʲi   ma ˈjɛi   vʲis ˈnɨ
златые   дни,   златые   дни   моей   весны!
golden   days,   golden   days   mine   of springtime!

RIGOLETTO

music: Giuseppe Verdi
libretto: Francesco Maria Piave (after Victor Hugo's drama *Le Roi s'Amuse*)

La donna è mobile

la   ˈdɔn: na   ɛ   ˈmɔ bi le
La   donna   è   mobile
the   woman   is   variable

kwal   ˈpju ma   al   ˈvɛn to
qual   piuma   al   vento;
like   feather   in the   wind

ˈmu ta   dat: ˈtʃɛn to
muta   d'accento
she changes   in word

e   di   pen ˈsjɛ ɾo
e   di   pensiero.
and   in   thought

ˈsɛm pre   un   a ˈma bi le
Sempre   un   amabile
always   a   lovable

led: ˈdʒa dro   ˈvi zo
leggiadro   viso,
pretty   face

in	'pjan to	o	in	'ri zo
in	**pianto**	**o**	**in**	**riso,**
in	*weeping*	*or*	*in*	*laughter*

ε	men tsoɲ:	'ɲɛ ɾo
è	**menzognero.**	
is	*untruthful*	

ε	'sɛm pre	'mi ze ɾo
È	**sempre**	**misero**
is	*always*	*miserable*

ki	a	'lɛi	saf: 'fi da
chi	**a**	**lei**	**s'affida,**
he who	*to*	*her*	*entrusts*

ki	le	kon 'fi da
chi	**le**	**confida**
he who	*her*	*relies on*

mal	'ka u to	il	'kɔ ɾe
mal	**cauto**	**il**	**core!**
not	*cautious*	*the*	*heart*

pur	'ma i	non	'sɛn te si
Pur	**mai**	**non**	**sentesi**
yet	*never*	*not*	*feels himself*

fe 'li tʃe	ap: 'pjɛ no
felice	**appieno**
happy	*fully*

ki	su	kwel	'se no
chi	**su**	**quel**	**seno**
he who	*upon*	*that*	*breast*

non	'li ba	a 'mo ɾe
non	**liba**	**amore!**
not	*tastes*	*love*

LE ROI D'YS

music: Edouard Lalo
libretto: Edouard Blau (after a Breton legend)

Vainement, ma bien-aimée

pɥi̯ skɔ̃	nœ	pø	fle ʃir
Puisqu'on	**ne**	**peut**	**fléchir**
since one	*not*	*is able*	*to move to pity*

sɛ	ʒa lu zœ	gar dje nœ
ces	**jalouses**	**gardiennes,**
those	*jealous*	*guardians*

a	lɛ se mwa	kɔ̃ te
ah,	**laissez-moi**	**conter**
ah	*allow me*	*to relate*

mɛ	pɛ nœ	e	mɔ̃	ne mwa
mes	**peines**	**et**	**mon**	**émoi!**
my	*pains*	*and*	*my*	*emotion*

vɛ nœ mã   ma   bjɛ̃‿nɛ me œ
Vainement,   ma   bien-aimée,
in vain   my   beloved one

ɔ̃   krwɑ   mœ   de zɛ spe re
on   croit   me   désespérer;
one   believes   me   to make desperate

prɛ dœ   ta   pɔr tœ   fɛr me œ
près de   ta   porte   fermée
near to   your   door   closed

ʒœ   vø‿   zã kɔr   dœ mœ re
je   veux   encor   demeurer!
I   wish   still   to stay

lɛ   sɔ lɛj   pu rɔ̃   se tɛ̃ drœ
Les   soleils   pourront   s'éteindre,
the   suns   will be able   to die out

lɛ   nɥi   rã pla se   lɛ   ʒur
les   nuits   remplacer   les   jours,
the   nights   to replace   the   days

sã   ta ky ze   e   sã   mœ   plɛ̃ drœ
sans   t'accuser   et   sans   me   plaindre.
without   you to accuse   and   without   me   to complain

la   ʒœ   rɛs tœ re   tu ʒur
Là   je   resterai,   toujours!
there   I   shall remain   always

ʒœ   lœ   se   tɔ̃‿   nɑ‿   mɛ   du sœ
Je   le   sais,   ton   âme   est   douce,
I   it   know   your   soul   is   sweet

e   lœ rœ   bjɛ̃ to   vjɛ̃ dra
et   l'heure   bientôt   viendra
and   the hour   soon   will come

u   la   mɛ̃   ki   mœ   rœ pu sœ
où   la   main   qui   me   repousse
when   the   hand   which   me   repels

vɛr   la   mjɛ nœ   sœ tã dra
vers   la   mienne   se tendra!
toward   the   mine   will reach out

nœ   swa   pɑ   tro   tar di‿
Ne   sois   pas   trop   tardive
not   be   [not]   too   tardy

va   tœ lɛ se‿   ra tã drir
à   te laisser   attendrir!
to   yourself let   to soften

si   ro zɛn   bjɛ̃ to   na ri vœ
Si   Rozenn   bientôt   n'arrive,
if   Rozenn   soon   not arrives

ʒœ   vɛ   e lɑs   mu rir
je   vais,   hélas,   mourir!
I   am going   alas   to die

LA TRAVIATA

music: Giuseppe Verdi
libretto: Francesco Maria Piave (after the play *La Dame aux Camélias* by Alexandre Dumas fils)

De' miei bollenti spiriti

'lun dʒe da 'lɛ i per me non va di 'lɛt: to
Lunge da lei per me non v'ha diletto!
far from her for me not there is pleasure

vo 'la ɾon dʒa tre 'lu ne
Volaron già tre lune
they fly by already three lunar months

dak: 'ke la 'mi a vi o 'let: ta
dacchè la mia Violetta
since the my Violetta

'a dʒi per me laʃ: 'ʃɔ do 'vit: tsje a 'mo ɾi
agi per me lasciò, dovizie, amori
comforts for me she left wealths loves

e le pom 'po ze 'fɛ ste
e le pompose feste,
and the pompous festivities

o 'vaʎ: ʎi o 'mad: dʒi av: 'vet: tsa
ov'agli omaggi avvezza,
where to the compliments accustomed

ve 'de a 'skja vo tʃa 'skun
vedea schiavo ciascun
she saw slave everyone

di 'su a bel: 'let: tsa
di sua bellezza.
of her beauty

e 'dor kon 'tɛn ta iŋ 'kwe sti a 'mɛ ni 'lwɔ gi
Ed or contenta in questi ameni luoghi
and now content in these pleasant surroundings

'tut: to 'skɔr da per me
tutto scorda per me.
all she forgets for me

kwi 'prɛs: so a 'lɛ i 'i o ri 'naʃ: ʃer mi 'sɛn to
Qui presso a lei io rinascer mi sento,
here beside her I to be reborn [I] myself feel

e dal 'sof: fjo da 'mor ri dʒe ne 'ɾa to
e dal soffio d'amor rigenerato
and by the breath of love regenerated

'skɔr do ne 'ga u di 'swɔ i
scordo ne' gaudi suoi
I forget in [the] joys its

'tut: to il pas: 'sa to
tutto il passato.
all the past

de   'mjɛ i   bol: 'lɛn ti   'spi ɾi ti
De'   miei   bollenti   spiriti
of [the]   my   boiling   spirits

il   dʒo va 'ni le   ar 'do ɾe
il   giovanile   ardore
the   youthful   ardor

'el: la   tem 'prɔ   kol   'pla tʃi do
ella   temprò   col   placido
she   tempered   with the   peaceful

sor: 'ri zo   del: la 'mor
sorriso   dell'amor!
smile   of the love

dal   di   ke   'dis: se
Dal   dì   che   disse:
from the   day   that   she said

'vi ve ɾe   'i o   'vɔʎ: ʎo   a   te   fe 'del   si
vivere   io   voglio   a   te   fedel,   sì,
to live   I   [I] want   to   you   faithful   yes

del: 'lu ni vɛr so   im: 'mɛ mo ɾe
dell'universo   immemore
of the universe   unmindful

'i o   'vi vo   'kwa zi   in   tʃɛl
io   vivo   quasi   in   ciel.
I   [I] live   almost   in   heaven

a   si
Ah   sì.
ah   yes

DIE ZAUBERFLÖTE

music: Wolfgang Amadeus Mozart
libretto: Emanuel Schikaneder (loosely based on a fairy tale by Wieland)

Dies Bildnis ist bezaubernd schön

di:s   'bɪlt nɪs   ɪst⇨   bə 'tsaʊ bɐnt   ʃøːn
Dies   Bildnis   ist   bezaubernd   schön,
This   portrait   is   enchantingly   beautiful,

vi: nɔx   kaɪn   'aʊ gə   je: gə 'ze:n
wie   noch   kein   Auge   je   gesehn!
as   so far   no   eye   ever   beheld!

ɪç   fy:⇨   ⇨lɛs   vi: di:s   'gœt⇨ tɐ 'bɪlt
Ich   fühl'   es,   wie   dies   Götterbild
I   feel   it   how   this   godlike image

maɪn   hɛrts   mɪt   'nɔy ɐ   're: gʊŋ   fʏllt
mein   Herz   mit   neuer   Regung   füllt.
my   heart   with   new   emotion   fills.

di:s   'ɛt vas   kan⇨   ⇨nɪç   tsva:r   nɪçt⇨   'nɛn⇨ nən
Dies   Etwas   kann   ich   zwar   nicht   nennen;
This   something   can   I   really   not   name;

dɔx   fy:⇨   ⇨lɪç⇨   ⇨s hi:ᵃ   vi: 'fɔy ɐ   'brɛn⇨ nən
doch   fühl   ich's   hier   wie   Feuer   brennen.
but   feel   I it   here   like   fire   burn.

zɔll	diː	ɛm ˈpfɪn dʊŋ	ˈliː bə	zaɪn
Soll	**die**	**Empfindung**	**Liebe**	**sein?**
Could	*this*	*sensation*	*love*	*be?*

ja ja	diː	ˈliː bə	ɪsts	al⇨ laɪn
Ja, ja!	**Die**	**Liebe**	**ist's**	**allein.**
Oh yes!	*(The)*	*love*	*is it*	*alone.*

oː	vɛn⇨	⇨nɪç	ziː	nuːᵃ	ˈfɪn dən	ˈkœnn tə
O	**wenn**	**ich**	**sie**	**nur**	**finden**	**könnte!**
Oh,	*if*	*I*	*her*	*only*	*find*	*could!*

oː vɛnn	ziː	dɔx	ʃoːn	foːᵃ	miːᵃ	ˈʃtɛːn də
O wenn	**sie**	**doch**	**schon**	**vor**	**mir**	**stände!**
Oh, if	*she*	*already*	*only*	*before*	*me*	*stood!*

ɪç	ˈvʏr də	varm	ʊnt	raɪn
Ich	**würde...**	**warm**	**und**	**rein—**
I	*would...*	*warmly*	*and*	*chastely—*

vas	ˈvʏr də	ɪç
was	**würde**	**ich?**
What	*would*	*I*

ɪç	ˈvʏr də	ziː	fɔll	ɛnt⇨ tsʏk⇨kən
Ich	**würde**	**sie**	**voll**	**Entzücken**
I	*would*	*her*	*full of*	*delight*

an	diː zən	ˈhaɪ sən	ˈbuː zən	drʏk⇨ kən
an	**diesen**	**heißen**	**Busen**	**drücken,**
to	*this*	*burning*	*breast*	*press*

ʊnt	ˈeː viç	ˈvɛː rə	ziː	dann	maɪn
und	**ewig**	**wäre**	**sie**	**dann**	**mein.**
and	*eternally*	*would be*	*she*	*than*	*mine.*

Un'aura amorosa

from
COSÌ FAN TUTTE

Wolfgang Amadeus Mozart

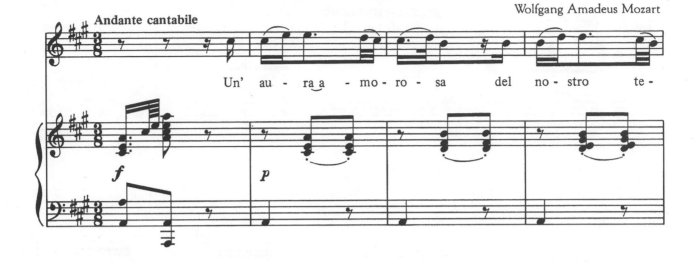

Un' au - ra a - mo - ro - sa del no - stro te -

so - ro un dol - ce ri - sto - ro al cor____ por - ge -

rà.____ Un' au - ra a - mo - ro - sa del no - stro te -

so - ro un dol - ce ri - sto - ro al cor___ por - ge -

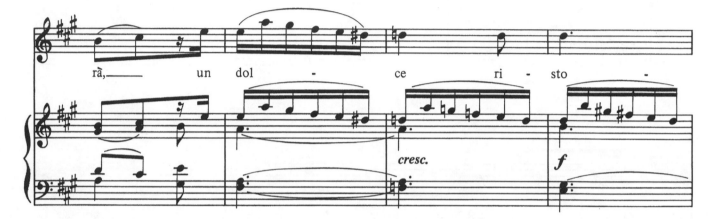

rà,___ un dol - ce ri - sto -

ro al___ cor por - ge - rà... al

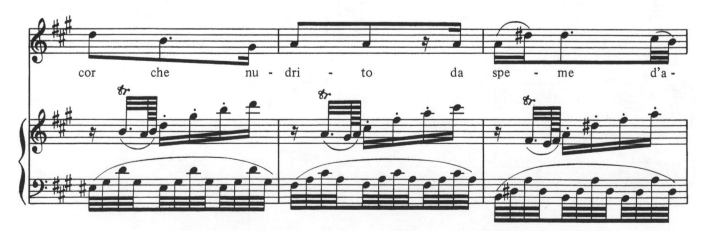

cor che nu - dri - to da spe - me d'a -

mo - re,   da   spe - me   d'a - mo - re,   d'un e - sca mi -

glio - re____ bi - so - gno_ non ha,   d'un e sca mi -

glio - re   bi - so - gno   non   ha,   bi - so - gno   non

ha,   bi - so - gno   non ha.   Un' au - ra_a - mo - ro - sa   del

34

no - stro te - so - ro un dol - ce ri - sto - ro al cor por-ge -

rà.____ Un' au - ra a - mo - ro - sa del no - stro te - so - ro un

dol - ce ri - sto - ro al cor por - ge - rà,____ un dol -

ce ri - sto - ro al____ cor por - ge -

rà, al cor por ge - rà, al cor por ge -

rà, un dol - ce ri - sto - ro al cor

por - ge - rà.

Dalla sua pace

from
DON GIOVANNI

secco recitativo
DON OTTAVIO:

Wolfgang Amadeus Mozart

Co-me mai cre-der deg-gio di sì ne-ro de-lit-to ca - pa-ce un ca-va-lie - re!

secco recitativo

Ah, di-sco-pri-re il ve-ro o-gni mez - zo si cer-chi; io sen-to in pet-to e di spo-so e d'a -

mi-co il do-ver che mi par-la: di's-in-gan-nar la vo-glio, o ven-di-car - la!

*Appoggiatura recommended

Andantino sostenuto

Dal - la sua pa - ce la mi - a di - pen - de.

Quel che a lei pia - ce_ vi - ta mi_ ren - de;

quel che le in - cre - sce mor - te mi dà, mor -

te, mor - te mi dà. S'el - la so -

spi - ra, so - spi - ro an-ch'i - o. È mia quell'

i - ra; quel pian - to è mi - o, e non ho be - ne

s'el - la non l'ha, e non ho be - ne s'el - la non

l'ha, e non ho be - ne s'el - la non l'ha.

Dal - la sua pa - ce la mi-a di - pen - de. Quel che a lei

pia - ce vi - ta mi ren - de; quel che le in - cre - sce

cresc. *mf*

mor - te mi dà, mor - te, mor - te mi

f *p* *cresc.* *p*

dà. Dal-la sua pa - ce la mia di - pen - de. Quel che a lei pia - ce vi - ta mi

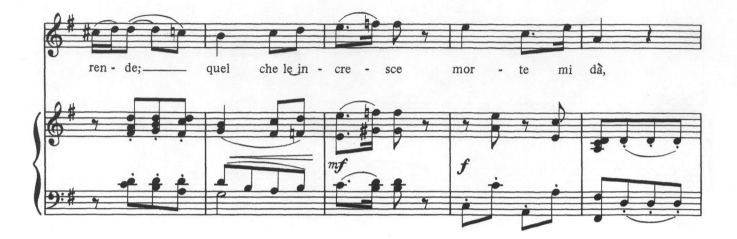

ren - de; _____ quel che le in - cre - sce mor - te mi dà,

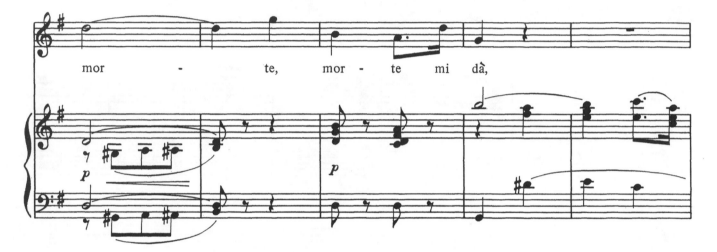

mor - te, mor - te mi dà,

mor - te mi dà, quel che le in - cre - sce _____ mor - te mi dà.

Il mio tesoro

from
DON GIOVANNI

Wolfgang Amadeus Mozart

DON OTTAVIO:

Il mio te - so - ro in - tan - to   an -

da - te, an - da - te a con - so - lar,

e del bel ci - glio il pian - to cer - ca - te di a - sciu -

gar, _____ cer - ca - te, cer - ca - te, cer -

ca - te di a - sciu - gar, _____ cer -

ca - - - - - -

- - te___ di___ a - sciu - gar.

Di - te - le che i suoi tor - ti a ven - di - car io

va - do,   a _____ ven-di-car ____ io ____

va - do: che sol   di stra - gi_e

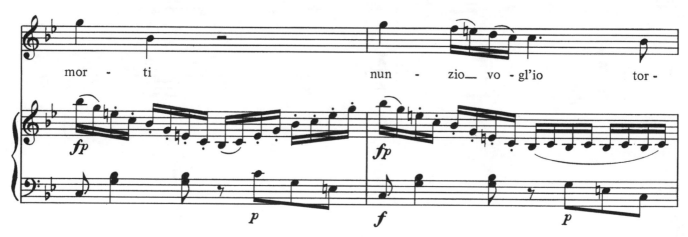

mor - ti   nun - zio __ vo-gl'io   tor -

nar,   nun -   zio vo-gl'i - o tor -

an - da - te, an - da - te a — con - so -

lar, e del bel — ci - gl'io il pian - to cer -

ca - te — di a - sciu - gar, cer - ca - te, cer -

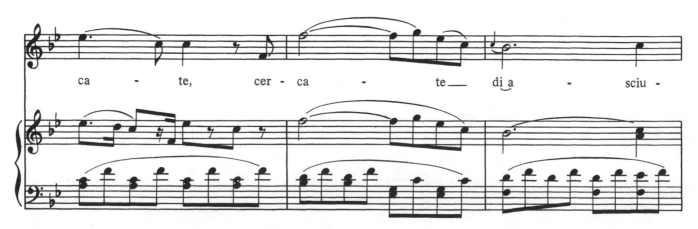

ca - te, cer - ca - te — di a - sciu -

47

gar,_____ cer - ca _____ _____

_____ - te_____ di_ a - sciu -gar.

Di - te-le_ che_i suoi tor - ti a ven-di-car io

va - do, a_ ven-di-car_ i - o va - _____

do: che sol di stra - gi e

mor - ti nun - zio vo-gl'i - o tor -

nar, _____ nun - zio,

nun - zio vo - gl'io _____ tor - nar, che

sol di stra - gi_e mor - ti

nun - zio vo - gl'io tor - nar, sì,

nun - zio vo-gl'io tor - nar!

Quanto è bella

from
L' ELISIR D'AMORE

Gaetano Donizetti

NEMORINO:

Quan-to è bel - la, quan-to è ca - ra! Più la ve - do e più— mi—

pia - ce, ma in quel cor non son— ca - pa - ce lie - ve af-

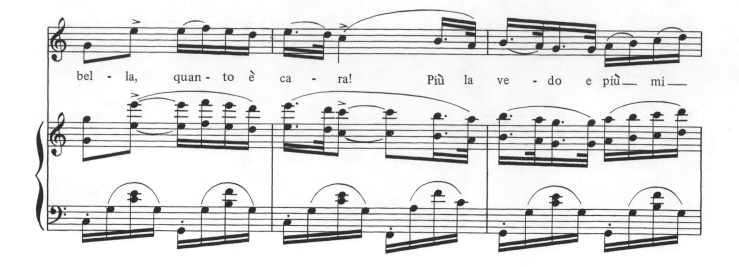

bel - la, quan- to è ca - ra! Più la ve - do e più__ mi__

pia - ce, ma in quel cor non son ca - pa - ce lie- ve af-

fet - to__ d'in - spi - rar. In quel cor non son ca - pa - ce lie- ve af- fet - to d'in - spi-

53

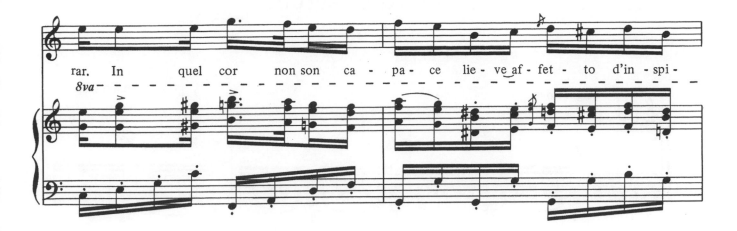

rar. In quel cor non son ca - pa - ce lie - ve af - fet - to d'in - spi -

rar, lie - ve af - fet - to

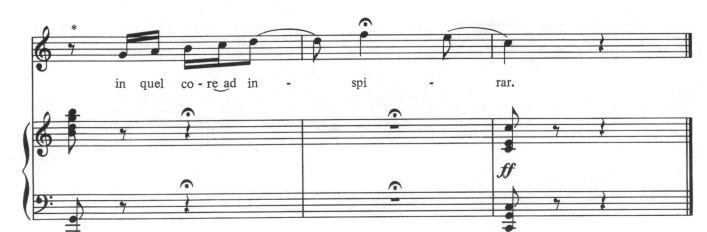

in quel co - re ad in - spi - rar.

*Optional Cadenza

non son ca - pa - ce, ah, non son ca - pa - ce lie-ve af-fet - to d'in - spi - rar.

Una furtiva lagrima

from

L' ELISIR D'AMORE

Gaetano Donizetti

U - na fur - ti - va

la - gri - ma   ne - gl'oc-chi suoi   spun - tò.

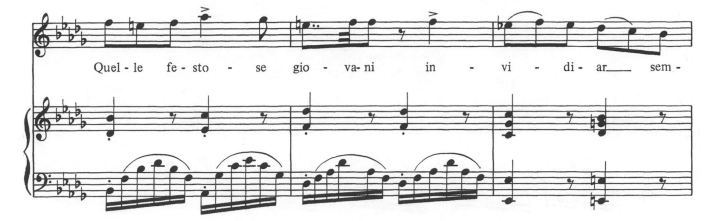

Quel - le fe - sto - se gio - va-ni in - vi - di - ar___ sem -

brò.   Che più cer - can - do io vo'?

Che più cer - can - do io vo'?   M'a - ma. Sì,

m'a - ma.___ Lo ve - do, lo ve - do.

Un so-lo i-stan - te i pal-pi-ti

del suo bel cor___ sen - tir! I miei so-spir con-

fon - de-re per po-co a' suoi___ so-spir! I

pal - pi-ti, i pal - pi-ti sen-tir, con-fon-de-re i miei co'suoi so-

spir!   Cie - lo, si può mo - rir;   di— più non—

chie-do, non chie - do.   Ah!   Cie - lo, si può, si può— mo -

rir;   di più— non— chie-do, non chie - -

do.

*This alternate cadenza has become traditional.

chie - - do. Si può mo-rir, si può mo-rir d'a - mor.

Lenski's Aria
from
EUGENE ONEGIN

Pyotr Il'yich Tchaikovsky

ЧТО ДЕНЬ ГРЯ-ДУ-ЩІЙ МНЕ ГО - ТО - ВИТЬ? Е -

ГО МОЙ ВЗОРЬ НА-ПРА-СНО ЛО - ВИТЬ; В ГЛУ - БО - КОЙ ТЬМЕ ТА - ИТ - СЯ ОНЬ!

НЕТЬ НУЖ-ДЫ, ПРАВЬ СУДЬ-БЫ ЗА - КОНЬ! ПА -

ДУ - ЛИ Я СТРЕ-ЛОЙ ПРОН - ЗЕН - НЫЙ, ИЛЬ МИ - МО ПРО-ЛЕ-ТИТЬ О-

НА, ВСЕ БЛА - ГО: БДЕ - НИ - Я И

poco riten.

СНА ПРИ-ХО - ДИТЬ ЧАСЬ О - ПРЕ-ДЕ - ЛЕН - НЫЙ! БЛА - ГО-СЛО - ВЕНЬ И ДЕНЬ ЗА - БОТ.

БЛА - ГО-СЛО-ВЕНЬ И ТЬМЫ _____ ПРИ - ХОДЬ!

poco string.

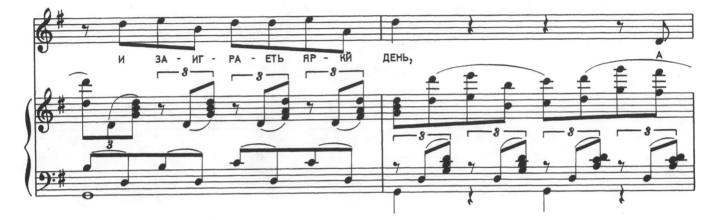

62

63

УР - НОЙ И ДУ - МАТЬ: ОНЬ МЕ - НЯ ЛЮ - БИЛЬ! ___

ОНЬ МНЕ Е - ДИ - НОЙ ПО - СВЯ - ТИЛЬ РАЗ-СВЕТЬ ПЕ -

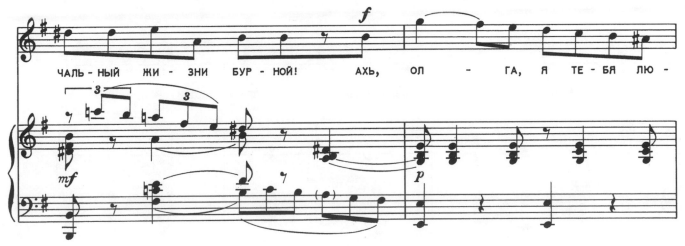

ЧАЛЬ - НЫЙ ЖИ - ЗНИ БУР - НОЙ! АХЬ, ОЛ - ГА, Я ТЕ - БЯ ЛЮ -

БИЛЬ, ___ ТЕ - БЕ ___ Е - ДИ - НОЙ ПО - СВЯ -

64

65

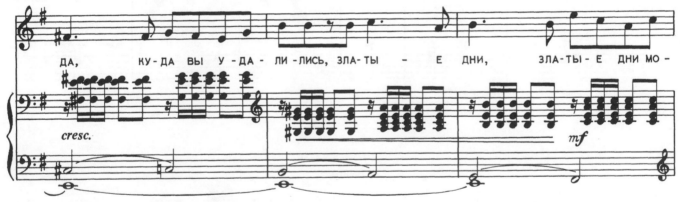

La donna è mobile

from
RIGOLETTO

Giuseppe Verdi

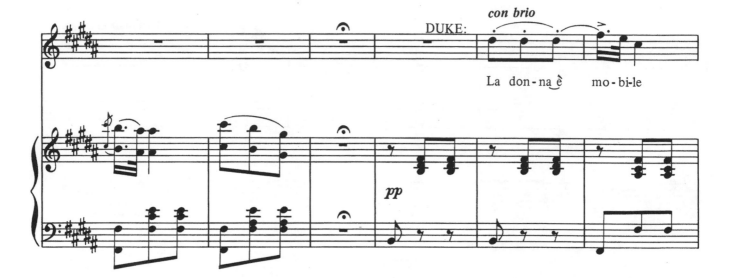

La don-na è mo-bi-le

qual piu-ma al ven-to; mu-ta d'ac-cen-to e di pen-

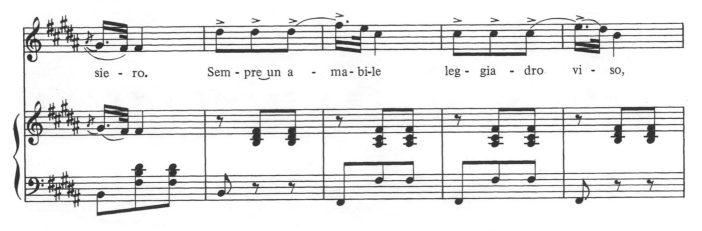

sie - ro.   Sem - pre_un a - ma - bi-le   leg - gia - dro   vi - so,

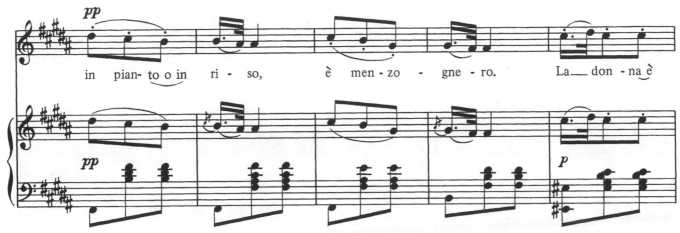

in   pian-to_o in   ri - so,   è   men - zo - gne - ro.   La__ don - na_è

mo - bil   quai__piu-ma_al   ven - to;   mu - ta   d'ac - cen - to

e___ di   pen - sier,

e——— di pen - sier,   e,———

con forza

e—— di—— pen - sier.

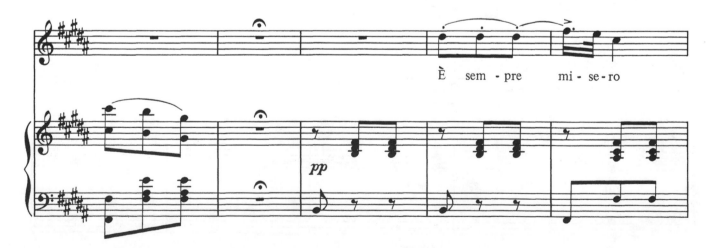

È sem - pre mi - se - ro

69

e ___ di pen - sier,

e ___ di pen - sier,   e, _____

e ___ di ___ pen - sier.

*This cadenza has become traditional; singers normally begin the held F♯ two measures later than written.

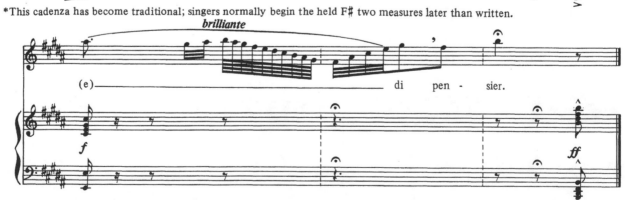

(e) _____ di pen - sier.

Vainement, ma bien-aimée

from
LE ROI D'YS

Édouard Lalo

72

Vai - ne - ment, _____ ma bien - ai -

mé - e, on croit me dé - ses - pé - rer;

près de ta por - te fer - mé - e je

veux _____ en - cor de - meu - rer!

Les so-leils pour - ront s'é - tein - dre,

les _ nuits rem-pla - cer les jours, sans t'ac-cu-ser et sans me plain - dre.

74

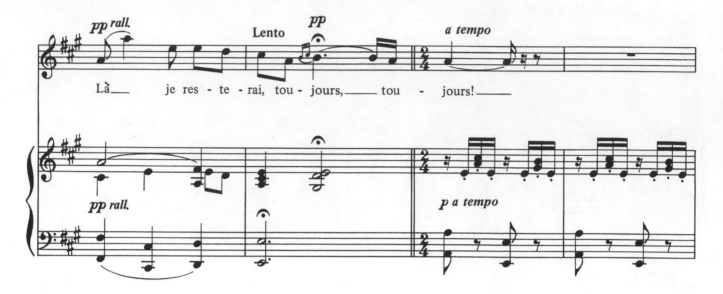

Là___ je res - te - rai, tou - jours,___ tou - jours!___

Je le sais,_____ ton âme est dou - ce, et

l'heu - re bien - tôt vien - dra où la main_____ qui me re -

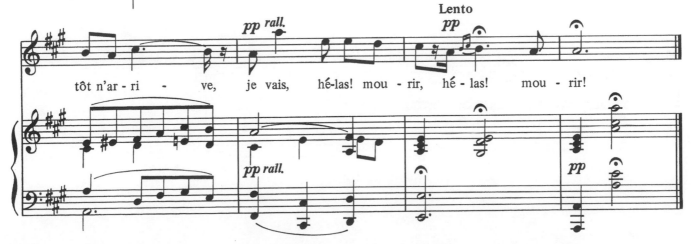

De' miei bollenti spiriti

from
LA TRAVIATA

Giuseppe Verdi

Allegro vivace (♩ = 132)

77

Andante

lez - za. Ed or con - ten - ta in que - sti_a - me - ni luo - ghi tut - to scor - da per

Adagio

me. Qui pres - so_a lei io ri - na - scer mi sen - to, e dal

sof - fio d'a - mor ri - ge - ne - ra - to scor-do ne' gau - di suo - i

tut - to il pas - sa - to.

80

Dies Bildnis ist bezaubernd schön

from

DIE ZAUBERFLÖTE

Wolfgang Amadeus Mozart

Dies Bild - nis ist be-zau-bernd

schön, wie noch kein Au - ge je ge - sehn! Ich

fühl' es, ich fühl' es, wie dies Göt - ter - bild mein

Herz _____ mit neu - er Re - gung __ füllt, mein

Herz _____ mit __ neu - er Re - gung __ füllt.

Dies __ Et - was kann ich zwar nicht

nen - nen; doch __ fühl ich's _ hier wie Feu - er bren - nen.

Soll die Emp-fin - dung__ Lie - be sein?   Soll__ die Emp-fin - dung

Lie - be sein?   Ja, ja!   Die Lie - be ist's al -

lein.   Die Lie - be,   die Lie - be,   die Lie - be

ist's _____ al - lein.

O wenn ich sie nur fin - den könn - te! O wenn sie doch schon vor mir

stän - de! Ich wür - de, wür - de...

warm und rein— was wür - de ich?

Ich wür - de sie___ voll___ Ent -

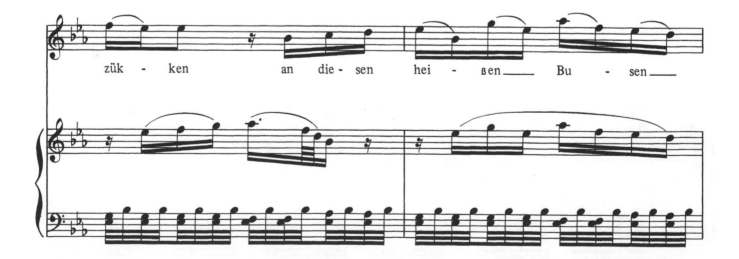

zük - ken an die - sen hei - ßen___ Bu - sen___

drück - en, und e - wig wä - re sie dann mein, und e - wig

wä - re sie dann mein, und e - wig wä - re sie dann

mein, e - wig wä - re sie dann mein, e - wig

wä - re sie dann mein.